SQL FOR BEGINNERS

A Simple Beginner's Guide For Learning The Fundamentals Of SQL

By: Technowledge

CONTENTS

INTRODUCTION

What is SQL?

SQL stands for Structured Query Language and is the lingua franca in the database world. SQL is a standard that is used by all database vendors and programmers to define, extract and access the information that is stored in databases.

SQL began life as an IBM creation but was standardized by the American National Standards Institute (ANSI) and the International Organization for Standardization (ISO) as ANSI/ISO SQL in 1988. Since then ANSI/ISO SQL standard continued to evolve. The ANSI-SQL group has since published three standards over the years:

1. SQL89 (SQL1)

2. SQL92 (SQL2)

3. SQL99 (SQL3)

SQL is a query language. It is English-like and easy to use.

However, although there are more than 90 SQL reserved words, most programmers seldom use more than the following handful of commands - SELECT, INSERT, UPDATE, DELETE, FROM, WHERE, HAVING, BETWEEN, LIKE, OR, AND, NOT, IN, ORDER, GROUP and BY.

For example, if you had a database table named "employees" and you wanted to retrieve all records where the employee has the last name "goodman", you would use the following SQL statement:

SELECT * FROM employees WHERE lastname = 'goodman';

There are many different categories of SQL statements but the basic ones which all programmers should be familiar with are the SQL statements that:

1. Create tables and manipulate their definitions

2. Query the table data

3. Manipulate the table data

SQL is predominantly used by 2 types of users - programs and humans (keying in the commands through a database client) - to pass instructions to databases. SQL commands can be keyed into a database client like the MySQL Query Browser or the SQL Server Enterprise Manager and executed to either return a result or modify records in the database.

SQL can also be used in conjunction with programming language or scripting language like Microsoft Visual Basic or PHP to communicate with the database.

Although SQL is a world standard, it is unfortunate that most database vendors have come up with different dialects and variations. This is because every database vendor wants to differentiate their database products from the crowd.

One good example is Microsoft SQL Server's TRANSACT-SQL. TRANSACT-SQL is a superset of SQL and is designed for use only with Microsoft SQL Server. Although it does make programming much easier for software developers, it is not compliant with other databases like Oracle or MySQL - making TRANSACT-SQL programs non database-portable.

As such, although many of these features are powerful and robust, it is good practice to exercise caution and limit your SQL use to be compliant with the ANSI/ISO SQL standards and ODBC-Compliant.

CHAPTER 1: WHAT IS SQL RDBMS?

A Relational Database Management System is a piece of software used to store and manage data in database objects called tables. A relational database table is a tabular data structure arranged in columns and rows.

The table columns also known as table fields have unique names and different attributes defining the column type, default value, indexes and several other column characteristics. The rows of the relational database table are the actual data entries.

SQL RDBMS

The most popular RDBMS are MS SQL Server from Microsoft, Oracle from Oracle Corp., DB2 from IBM, MySQL from MySQL, and MS Access from Microsoft. Most commercial database vendors have developed their proprietary SQL extension based on ANSI-SQL standard.

For example the SQL version utilized by MS SQL Server is called Transact-SQL or simply T-SQL, The Oracle's version is called PL/SQL (short for Procedural Language/SQL), and MS Access use Jet-SQL.

What can you do with SQL?

o SQL queries are used to retrieve data from database tables. The SQL queries use the SELECT SQL keyword which is part of the Data Query Language (DQL). If we have a table called "Orders" and you want to select all entries where the order value is greater than $100 ordered by the order value, you can do it with the following SQL SELECT query:

SELECT   OrderID,   ProductID,   CustomerID,   OrderDate, OrderValue

FROM Orders

WHERE OrderValue > 200

ORDER BY OrderValue;

The FROM SQL clause specifies from which table(s) we are retrieving data. The WHERE SQL clause specifies search criteria (in our case to retrieve only records with OrderValue greater than $200). The ORDER BY clause specifies that the returned data has to be order by the OrderValue column. The WHERE and ORDER BY clauses are optional.

o You can manipulate data stored in relational database tables, by using the INSERT, UPDATE and DELETE SQL keywords. These three SQL commands are part of the Data Manipulation Language (DML).

-- To insert data into a table called "Orders" you can use a SQL statement similar to the one below:

INSERT INTO Orders (ProductID, CustomerID, OrderDate, OrderValue)

VALUES (10, 108, '12/12/2007', 99.95);

-- To modify data in a table you can use a statement like this:

UPDATE Orders

SET OrderValue = 199.99

WHERE CustomerID = 10 AND OrderDate = '12/12/2007';

-- To delete data from database table use a statement like the one below:

DELETE Orders

WHERE CustomerID = 10;

o You can create, modify or delete database objects (example of database objects are database tables, views, stored procedures, etc.), by using the CREATE, ALTER and DROP SQL keywords. These three SQL keywords are part of the Data Definition Language (DDL). For example to create table "Orders" you can use the following SQL statement:

CREATE Orders

(

OrderID INT IDENTITY(1, 1) PRIMARY KEY,

ProductID INT,

CustomerID ID,

OrderDate DATE,

OrderValue Currency

)

o You can control database objects privileges by using the GRANT and REVOKE keywords, part of the Data Control Language (DCL). For example to allow the user with username "User1" to select data from table "Orders" you can use the following SQL statement:

GRANT SELECT ON Orders TO User1

CHAPTER 2: WHY SQL IS IMPORTANT?

Today every software professional needs at least a basic understanding of how SQL works. If you are new to SQL, you might feel overwhelmed and confused in the beginning, but as you progress you will discover how powerful and elegant SQL is.

Network programs are now bigger and more flexible. More often than not, the basic scheme of operations are mostly a combination of scripts that handle the control of a database.

Because of the diversity of languages and existing databases, the way to "talk" between each other can often be complicated and challenging, luckily for us, the presence of standards that allow us to perform the usual procedures through a widespread form makes this confusing job more straightforward.

That's what Structured Query Language (SQL) is centered on, which happens to be nothing but an international standard language of communication within databases.

That is why, the Structured Query Language (SQL) is truly a standardized language that allows all of us to implement any language e.g. ASP or PHP, in conjunction with any specific database e.g. MySQL, SQL Server, MS Access.

SQL was manufactured by IBM during the1970's, in the beginning it was called SEQUEL (Structure English Query Language). Years later, Microsoft and Oracle also started using SEQUEL.

Their global recognition and used grew and then the term SEQUEL was changed. In 1986, the term SEQUEL was standardized by the American National Standards Institute (ANSI) to SQL. In other words, they ditched the world "English" from the term.

Until this day, there are lots of users who refuse to refer to it as SQL, to these people, SEQUEL certainly is the right name for this international standardized database language. SQL has additionally been revised in 1989 and then 1992 (SQL-92).

Ever since,SQL has undergone many revisions to enhance their standardization.

SQL is surely an international standardized language, but that does not mean that is similar for each database. Believe it or not, some databases execute particular functions that will not always run in others.

That's the reason why every company that delivers database products, for instance Microsoft and Oracle, have their own certification process ensuring that those that takes the certification exam are very well prepared and understand the differences between the various models of SQL. Their knowledge is focus on their own unique specific version of SQL.

SQL is not simply relevant because of the ability to standardized an otherwise confusing language, it provides two other unique characteristics. On one hand, it really is tremendously flexible and powerful. On the other hand, it is very accessible which makes it simpler to master.

There are many databases products that support SQL, however, two of the biggest and most widely used are Microsoft SQL server and Oracle database.

Each company that offers database product has their own path to become an "expert". For example, Microsoft offers a variety of certifications to ensure that every Microsoft SQL Certified meets their criteria. Oracle does the same thing with their Certification process.

CHAPTER 3: BASICS OF SQL INJECTION

SQL Injection is one of the many web attack mechanisms used by hackers to steal data from organisations. It is perhaps one of the most common application layer attack techniques used today.

Web applications allow legitimate website visitors to submit and retrieve data to/from a database over the Internet using their preferred web browser.

Databases are central to modern websites - they store data needed for websites to deliver specific content to visitors and render information to customers, suppliers, employees and a host of stakeholders.

User credentials, financial and payment information, company statistics may all be resident within a database and accessed by legitimate users through off-the-shelf and custom web applications. Web applications and databases allow you to regularly run your business.

SQL Injection is the hacking technique which attempts to pass SQL commands through a web application for execution by the backend database. If not santised properly, web applications may result in SQL Injection attacks that allow hackers to view information from the database and/or even wipe it out.

Such features as login pages, support and product request forms, feedback forms, search pages, shopping carts and the general delivery of dynamic content, shape modern websites and provide businesses with the means necessary to communicate with prospects and customers.

These website features are all examples of web applications which may be either purchased off-the-shelf or developed as bespoke programs.

These website features are all susceptible to SQL Injection attacks.

SQL Injection: A Simple Example

Take a simple login page where a legitimate user would enter his username and password combination to enter a secure area to view his personal details or upload his comments in a forum.

When the legitimate user submits his details, an SQL query is generated from these details and submitted to the database for verification. If valid, the user is allowed access.

In other words, the web application that controls the login page will communicate with the database through a series of planned commands so as to verify the username and password combination. On verification, the legitimate user is granted appropriate access.

Through SQL Injection, the hacker may input specifically crafted SQL commands with the intent of bypassing the login form barrier and seeing what lies behind it. This is only possible if the inputs are not properly sanitised (i.e., made invulnerable) and sent directly with the SQL query to the database. SQL Injection vulnerabilities provide the means for a hacker to communicate directly to the database.

The technologies vulnerable to this attack are dynamic script languages including ASP, ASP.NET, PHP, JSP, and CGI. All an attacker needs to perform an SQL Injection hacking attack is a web browser, knowledge of SQL queries and creative guess work to important table and field names. The sheer simplicity of SQL Injection has fuelled its popularity.

Why is it possible to pass SQL queries directly to a database that is hidden behind a firewall and any other security mechanism?

Firewalls and similar intrusion detection mechanisms provide little or no defense against full-scale SQL Injection web attacks.

Since your website needs to be public, security mechanisms will allow public web traffic to communicate with your web application/s (generally over port 80/443). The web application has open access to the database in order to return (update) the requested (changed) information.

In SQL Injection, the hacker uses SQL queries and creativity to get to the database of sensitive corporate data through the web application.

SQL or Structured Query Language is the computer language that allows you to store, manipulate, and retrieve data stored in a relational database (or a collection of tables which organise and structure data).

SQL is, in fact, the only way that a web application (and users) can interact with the database. Examples of relational databases include Oracle, Microsoft Access, MS SQL Server, MySQL, and Filemaker Pro, all of which use SQL as their basic building blocks.

SQL commands include SELECT, INSERT, DELETE and

DROP TABLE. DROP TABLE is as ominous as it sounds and in fact will eliminate the table with a particular name.

In the legitimate scenario of the login page example above, the SQL commands planned for the web application may look like the following:

SELECT count(*)

FROM users_list_table

WHERE username='FIELD_USERNAME'

AND password='FIELD_PASSWORD"

In plain English, this SQL command (from the web application) instructs the database to match the username and password input by the legitimate user to the combination it has already stored.

Each type of web application is hard coded with specific SQL queries that it will execute when performing its legitimate functions and communicating with the database.

If any input field of the web application is not properly sanitised, a hacker may inject additional SQL commands that broaden the range of SQL commands the web application will execute, thus going beyond the original intended design and function.

A hacker will thus have a clear channel of communication (or, in layman terms, a tunnel) to the database irrespective of all the intrusion detection systems and network security equipment installed before the physical database server.

Is my database at risk to SQL Injection?

SQL Injection is one of the most common application layer attacks currently being used on the Internet. Despite the fact that it is relatively easy to protect against SQL Injection, there are a large number of web applications that remain vulnerable.

It may be difficult to answer the question whether your web site and web applications are vulnerable to SQL Injection especially if you are not a programmer or you are not the person who has coded your web applications.

Our experience leads us to believe that there is a significant chance that your data is already at risk from SQL Injection.

Whether an attacker is able to see the data stored on the database or not, really depends on how your website is coded to display the results of the queries sent. What is certain is that the attacker will be able to execute arbitrary SQL Commands on the vulnerable system, either to compromise it or else to obtain information.

If improperly coded, then you run the risk of having your customer and company data compromised.

What an attacker gains access to also depends on the level of security set by the database. The database could be set to restrict to certain commands only. A read access normally is enabled for use by web application back ends.

Even if an attacker is not able to modify the system, he would still be able to read valuable information.

What is the impact of SQL Injection?

Once an attacker realizes that a system is vulnerable to SQL Injection, he is able to inject SQL Query / Commands through an input form field. This is equivalent to handing the attacker your database and allowing him to execute any SQL command including DROP TABLE to the database!

An attacker may execute arbitrary SQL statements on the vulnerable system. This may compromise the integrity of your database and/or expose sensitive information.

Depending on the back-end database in use, SQL injection vulnerabilities lead to varying levels of data/system access for the attacker. It may be possible to manipulate existing queries, to UNION (used to select related information from two tables) arbitrary data, use subselects, or append additional queries.

In some cases, it may be possible to read in or write out to files, or to execute shell commands on the underlying operating system.[break][break]Certain SQL Servers such as Microsoft SQL Server contain stored and extended procedures (database server functions). If an attacker can obtain access to these procedures it

Unfortunately the impact of SQL Injection is only uncoveredwhen the theft is discovered. Data is being unwittingly stolen through various hack attacks all the time. The more expert of hackers rarely get caught.

Example of a SQL Injection Attack

Here is a sample basic HTML form with two inputs, login and password.

http://testasp.acunetix.com/login.asp">

The easiest way for the login.asp to work is by building a database query that looks like this:

SELECT id

FROM logins

WHERE username = '$username'

AND password = '$password'

If the variables $username and $password are requested directly from the user's input, this can easily be compromised. Suppose that we gave "Joe" as a username and that the following string was provided as a password: anything' OR 'x'='x

SELECT id

FROM logins

WHERE username = 'Joe'

AND password = 'anything' OR 'x'='x'

As the inputs of the web application are not properly sanitised, the use of the single quotes has turned the WHERE SQL command into a two-component clause.

The 'x'='x' part guarantees to be true regardless of what the first part contains

This will allow the attacker to bypass the login form without actually knowing a valid username / password combination!

How do I prevent SQL Injection attacks?

Firewalls and similar intrusion detection mechanisms provide little defense against full-scale web attacks. Since your website needs to be public, security mechanisms will allow public web traffic to communicate with your databases servers through web applications. Isn't this what they have been designed to do?

Patching your servers, databases, programming languages and operating systems is critical but will in no way the best way to prevent SQL Injection Attacks.

CHAPTER 4: HARDENING YOUR WEB APPLICATIONS AGAINST SQL INJECTIONS

SQL injection is a technique that exploits a security vulnerability occurring in the database layer of a web application.

The vulnerability is present when user input is either incorrectly filtered for string literal escape characters embedded in SQL statements or user input is not strongly typed and thereby unexpectedly executed.

It is in fact an instance of a more general class of vulnerabilities that can occur whenever one programming or scripting language is embedded inside another.

"SQL Injection" is subset of the unverified/unsanitized user input vulnerability ("buffer overflows" are a different subset), and the idea is to convince the application to run SQL code that was not intended. If the application is creating SQL strings naively on the fly and then running them, it's straightforward to create some real surprises.

Many organization's web servers has been compromised just because of SQL Injections, including big names which I would not like to mention here, you can search it easily on Internet.

What is Blind SQL Injection?

This particular type of attack is called a blind SQL injection attack, because the attacker cannot take advantage of detailed error messages from the server or other sources of information about the application.

Getting the SQL syntax right is usually the trickiest part of the blind SQL injection process and may require a lot of trial and error. But, by adding more conditions to the SQL statement and evaluating the Web application's output, an attacker will eventually determine whether the application is vulnerable to SQL injection.

Blind SQL injection a special case that plays on the web developers or website owners sense of security. While they may think that everything on the server is tightly guarded a Blind SQL injection attack will silently be playing truth or consequences with the web server.

This type of attack though very time consuming is one that provides the most potentially damaging security hole. This is because an attacker gets not only access but is provided with an enormous amount of knowledge about the database and can potentially gain access to a servers file system.

This type of attack is one that is automated and requires good amount of setup to succeed. But once it is done it does not require a great deal of effort to repeat.

What is Error message SQL Injection?

Web applications commonly use SQL queries with client-supplied input in the WHERE clause to retrieve data from a database.

When a Web application executes such queries without validating or scanning the user-supplied data to ensure it's not harmful, a SQL injection attack can occur. By sending unexpected data, an attacker can generate and submit SQL queries to a web applications database.

A test for SQL injection vulnerabilities takes place by sending the application data that generates an invalid SQL query. If the server returns an error message, that information can be used to try to gain uncontrolled access to the database. This is the basis of one of the most popular SQL injection attacks.

Hiding error messages does not stop the SQL injection attack. What typically happens is the attacker will use the knowledge gained from the failure of this attack to change tactics. What they turn to is blind SQL injection.

Why SQL Injection?

When a web application fails to properly sanitize user-supplied input, it is possible for an attacker to alter the construction of backend SQL statements. When an attacker is able to modify a SQL statement, the process will run with the same permissions as the component that executed the command. (E.g. Database server, Web application server, Web server, etc.). The impact of this attack can allow attackers to gain total control of the database or even execute commands on the system.

When a machine has only port 80 opened, your most trusted vulnerability scanner cannot return anything useful, and you know that the admin always patch his server, this is the point where malicious hacker would turn to web hacking.

SQL injection is one of type of web hacking that require nothing but port 80 and it might just work even if the admin is patch-happy. It attacks on the web application (like ASP, JSP, PHP, CGI, etc) itself rather than on the web server or services running in the OS.

Types of SQL Injections:

There are four main categories of SQL Injection attacks against databases layer in Web Application

1. SQL Manipulation: manipulation is process of modifying the SQL statements by using various operations such as UNION .Another way for implementing SQL Injection using SQL Manipulation method is by changing the where clause of the SQL statement to get different results.

2. Code Injection: Code injection is process of inserting new SQL statements or database commands into the vulnerable SQL statement. One of the code injection attacks is to append a SQL Server EXECUTE command to the vulnerable SQL

statement. This type of attack is only possible when multiple SQL statements per database request are supported.

3. Function Call Injection: Function call injection is process of inserting various database function calls into a vulnerable SQL statement. These function calls could be making operating system calls or manipulate data in the database.

4. Buffer Overflows: Buffer overflow is caused by using function call injection. For most of the commercial and open source databases, patches are available. This type of attack is possible when the server is un-patched

SQL Injectin Prevention Techniques:

Mitigation of SQL injection vulnerability would be taking one of the two paths i.e. either using stored procedures along with callable statements or using prepared statements with dynamic SQL commands. Whichever way is adopted the data validation is must.

a. Input validation

Data sanitization is key. Best way to sanitize data is to use default deny, regular expression. Write specific filters. As far as possible use numbers, numbers and letters. If there is a need to include punctuation marks of any kind, convert them by

HTML encoding them. SO that " become """ or > becomes ">"

For instance if the user is submitting the E-mail address allow only @, -, . And _ in addition to numbers and letters to be used and only after they have been converted to their HTML substitutes

b. Use of prepared statement

The prepared statements should be used when the stored procedures cannot be used for whatever reason and dynamic SQL commands have to be used.

Use a Prepared Statement to send precompiled SQL statements with one or more parameters. Parameter place holders in a prepared statement are represented by the? And are called bind variables.

Prepared statement are generally immune to SQL Injection attacks as the database will use the value of the bind variable exclusively and not interpret the contents of the variable in any way. PL/SQL and JDBC allow for prepared statements. Prepared statements should be extensively used for both security and performance reasons.

c. Use minimum privileges

Make sure that application user has specific bare minimum rights on the database server. If the application user on the database uses ROOT/SA/dbadmin/dbo on the database then; it surely needs to be reconsidered if application user really needs such high amount of privileges or can they be reduced.

Do not give the application user permission to access system stored procedures allow access to the ones that are user created.

d. Stored procedures

To secure an application against SQL injection, developers must never allow client-supplied data to modify the syntax of SQL statements. In fact, the best protection is to isolate the web application from SQL altogether.

All SQL statements required by the application should be in stored procedures and kept on the database server. The application should execute the stored procedures using a safe interface such as Callable statements of JDBC or CommandObject of ADO

CHAPTER 5: MS SQL SERVER

Basically the MS SQL server is a management system that is created to work on different platforms like laptops or large servers. It is used as the backend system for many websites and it can help a number of users. There are many tools that help in maintenance of database and other tasks like programming.

Server: The database systems that are based on server are programmed in such a way that they run with the help of a central server and any number of users will be able to have access to the data at the same time with the help of an application.

The users can do multiple tasks like accessing the data, updating of data, and anything that they want to do. SQL server has features that help the application in all its functions.

Editions: There are many editions to SQL server and the user will choose the one that suits his requirements. For a free database management, the user will choose the Express or Compact edition. Some of the notable editions of SQL Server are:

Enterprise edition that has better availability and security for applications related to business; Standard edition that provides easy management of data management and to run departmental applications; workgroup edition for secured synchronization at the remote end, and to run branch applications;

Developer edition that can be made use of by one user in testing, developing, and demonstrating the programs in any number of systems; Web edition for web hosters; Express edition for learning purposes;

Compact edition meant for applications for desk tops, mobile services and web customers; and Evaluation edition for evaluating the purposes till the trial period is over.

Creating database: SQL server makes use of SQL Server Management Studio as the console for administration. It helps in creating databases, views, tables and so on, and to access the data, configuring the accounts, and to transfer data to other databases.

The Object Explorer guides the user to databases and to files. The user can get results by writing queries on data. Any amount of databases can be created with SQL server Management. After creating a database, the user can change the configuration of the database with the help of options available. Tables can also be created with the help of the options.

The user can control the type of data in each column and thus have integrity of the data maintained. Options such as editing and adding data are also available to the user. Re-entering the data is facilitated by writing a SQL script. The user can use and run the SQL query for inserting data, updating it or deleting it.

Query designer: This interface permits the user to create queries to be run against the database and to create queries which will include views or tables. It is very useful for the beginners who want to learn to use SQL as the syntax need not be remembered for creating queries.

View: A view in SQL server is store din the database and when run, it permits the user to see the outcome of it from multiple databases. This is particularly useful when many users want to access the data at various levels. They can have access to specific rows or columns of a table.

Stored procedures: These are of great value to the programmers when they work on databases. The programmers can make the procedures work from either the SQL Server management or any other application based on their requirement.

The advantages of the stored procedures are many, such as quicker execution, less traffic, and security. The user can configure SQL server security accounts, create linked servers, database maintenance, create scheduled jobs, replication, text search and many more.

Logins: SQL Server helps in creating user logins for every individual who wants to access the server. Based on the requirement of the user, the logins can be created to enable access.

Not everyone should be provided with access to server role. The server role is useful for performing any task in the server, create options of configuration, help in managing logins and permissions, and managing files.

Database Schema: It is a means of grouping the data and works as a container. The user can be assigned permission to a single schema so that he can access only the ones that they are permitted to. The schemes can be configured in a database. Linked Servers permit the users to connect to another server remotely.

MS SQL server is a very effective application useful in manipulating the data. Any website that has more data will make use of the server for effective functioning.

CHAPTER 6: SQL WEB HOSTING

Web Hosting is a service provided by a company that leases server space to companies or individuals that have web pages they want to display on the internet.

Web hosts provide the necessary bandwidth and technology to allow internet users to access these web pages. While anyone can create a web page, special servers dedicated to internet connectivity and hosting are required to make the web page active.

Therefore, SQL web hosting is a service that allows SQL databases to be hosted on the internet. SQL web hosting can be used to store database information on the web, allow offsite personal to access database management tools and provide detailed information to customers or clients.

Typical applications that use SQL databases are ERP (Enterprise Resource Planning) and CRM (Customer Relationship Management) programs.

What are the Benefits of SQL Web Hosting

There are several advantages to investing in an SQL web hosting service rather than relying on a standard web host. If you require a web based database, you will quickly come to appreciate these benefits:

Increased RAM and Bandwidth - Typically, database applications take up a lot of memory and server space. SQL web hosting services provide additional room for your database to evolve and grow over time.

SQL Administration Services - Because SQL web hosting services are dedicated to database hosting, they generally have the ability to offer advanced administration services to keep your database running smoothly and at optimum performance.

Technical Assistance and SQL Design - If you're new to SQL, many SQL web hosting services provide technical assistance and design packages for an additional cost when you purchase web hosting.

Things to Look for in a Quality SQL Web Hosting Service

Once you've decided to go with an SQL web host, you'll need to select a service. There are a lot of providers currently on the market, and sometimes it's difficult to tell them apart. A quality SQL web hosting service should offer you the following:

- Reliability
- Control Panel Options
- Technical Support
- Customer Support
- Multiple Hosting Plans

Overall, if you plan on maintaining a database online, your best option is to go with a web hosting service that has servers dedicated specifically to SQL applications.

Doing so will ensure that you get the most value out of your investment. SQL web hosting may cost a little more than standard hosting, but it's worth every penny.

CHAPTER 7: HOW TO RESTORE SQL DATABASE

MS SQL is an application produced by Microsoft which is used broadly for efficient data management by many organizations around the world and has really become an indispensable need of users all over.

SQL or the Structured Query Language helps the users to query the databases and also to easily retrieve information from databases that had been made already. In this MS SQL Server, the files are saved in .mdf file format.

With SQL functioning normally, data management is matchlessly easy but the real trouble arises for the users when any problem comes in this SQL Server.

If you are fed up of the SQL database corruption tension which is uncalled-for and also fed up of the unwanted impediment to your work because of it, then it is high time you get an SQL Server Restoring Database tool and immediately think - how to restore SQL database easily without any difficulty?

Only a reliable SQL restoring database software can be the ideal tension releaser that will take away the data loss fear and give way to complete satisfaction.

Why SQL gets corrupted?

Causes of SQL Server corruption are actually the reasons requiring the need for SQL recovery. The corruption is sudden and can happen unexpectedly due to several reasons like:

o Problem in hard drive

o Improper and strange system shutdown accidentally

o Virus or Trojan attack

o Software or hardware malfunction

o Incorrect String to multi-client database along with user deletion of Log file or database in "suspected" mode

o No free disk space available while the working of SQL Server

o While MS SQL database is running, disk controllers trying to access or copy the file

These are other such abrupt and unanticipated reasons lead to SQL corruption. It is impossible to turn the time back and avoid such thing to happen. Only possibility with the user is to think How to Restore SQL if he using SQL 2005 and how to restore SQL 2000 if he is using SQL Server 2000.

Errors appearing at the time of corruption

A user can get one of the following errors at the time of SQL corruption:

o Index '%ls' on '%ls' in database '%ls' may be corrupt because of expression evaluation changes in this release. Drop and re-create the index

o The file *.mdf is missing and needs to restore

o Server can't find the requested database table

o PageId in the page header = (0:0)

o Table Corrupt: Object ID 0, index ID 0, page ID (1:623)

o The process could not execute 'sp_replcmds' on server

o Internal error. Buffer provided to read column value is too small. Run DBCC CHECKDB to check for any corruption

o On changes table that was working .frm is locked

o The conflict occurred in database 'db_name', table 'table_name', column 'column_name'. The statement has been terminated

o Corruption error of indexes, stored procedures, triggers and database integrity table that should be there .MYI file is not

Know how to restore SQL easily without any difficulty?

First and foremost thing which a user is required to do is to judge whether there is a need for an outside SQL restoring database tool or not.

Professional help in the shape of an SQL Server recovery tool is required in case the user is getting any of the above errors because in that case recovery is only possible by using an outside software product. SysTools SQL recovery software is able to fix SQL server 2005 and 2000 database files easily without any difficulty.

Recovery happens easily because it requires no technical expertise and advanced system and software knowledge to perform successful SQL recovery. Just a few simple steps and you are through!

Recovery happens without any difficulty because the process is smooth and there will be no complications arising during the

SQL repair process. Also, the software is compatible with all the Windows Operating System versions like ME/NT/2000/XP/2003 and Vista.

CHAPTER 8: PL – SQL

PL/SQL is Oracle's Procedure language or programming language. It is very similar to other programming languages. We can record specific instructions in PL/SQL that tell our applications how to act.

PL/SQL has a wealth of tools that greatly enhance the processing of records. PL/SQL has looping statements that enable you to perform the same function a number of times.

It has condition logic that enables you to process records when certain conditions are met. It has cursors that enable you to move sets of records into memory and process them one at a time. PL/SQL code is grouped into structures called blocks.

If you create a stored procedure or package,you give the block of PL/SQL code a name; if the block of PL/SQL code is not given a name, then it is said to be an anonymous block. The examples in this chapter will feature anonymous blocks of

PL/SQL code; the following chapters in this section illustrate the creation of named blocks.

The main difference between SQL and PL/SQL is, In SQL's we can give one SQl command at a time but using PL/SQL we can give more than one SQL command at a time. Within a PL/SQL block, the first section is the Declarations section. Inside the Declarations section, you define the variables and cursors that the block will use.

The Declarations section starts with the keyword declare and ends when the Executable Commands section starts (as indicated by "begin"). The Executable Commands section is followed by the Exception Handling section; the exception keyword signals the start of the Exception Handling section. The PL/SQL block is terminated by the end keyword.

The structure of a typical PL/SQL block is shown in the following listing:

Declaration Part.

The declarative section such as variable declarations, cursor declarations etc.

Execution Part.

The Executable section. The complete programming codes are in this section.

Exception part

The exception handling section. If any error raised in the execution part, the controls just skip to the exception handling part. (Here the Declarative section and Exception handling section are optional. But the Execution section is must).

Declare

The Declarative Statements.

Begin

The Statements for execution.

Exception

The Error Handling Part

End;

Declarations Section

The Declarations section begins a PL/SQL block. The Declarations section starts with the declare keyword, followed by a list of variable and cursor definitions.

Executable Commands Section

In the Executable Commands section, you manipulate the variables and cursors declared in the Declarations section of your PL/SQL block. The Executable Commands section always starts with the keyword begin.

Exception Handling Section

When user-defined or system-related exceptions (errors) are encountered, the control of the PL/SQL block shifts to the Exception Handling section. Within the Exception Handling section, the when clause is used to evaluate which exception is to be "raised"-that is, executed.

If an exception is raised within the Executable Commands section of your PL/SQL block, the flow of commands immediately leaves the Executable Commands section and searches the Exception Handling section for an exception matching the error encountered. PL/SQL provides a lot of system-defined exceptions and allows you to add your own exceptions.

CHAPTER 9: ADVANCED SQL QUERIES

Database programming using SQL (Structured Query Language) is essential to build dynamic websites. Database servers are becoming more and more powerful by getting involved in computations rather than just passively storing data.

This means, some of the computational tasks are being taken care of by the database servers themselves. This has been made possible by the usage of advanced SQL query types. Let us discuss advanced SQL query types.

1. SQL Queries Using 'Group By' Clause

Consider that a table stores names of students, marks and subjects. Writing a simple query to retrieve the names and corresponding marks is not difficult at all. But, if the requirement is to show student names along with average marks across subjects, a simple SQL query will not be enough.

One way is to retrieve the entire data and perform the required computations in the business layer. If you had not known already, business layer is the one where server code (code written using languages like PHP,J2EE,Dot Net) resides. But, if you know to write queries having 'Group By' clause, you could very well do the computations in the database layer itself.

2. SQL Triggers

Queries are usually invoked by server programming languages like PHP,J2EE etc. However, there could be times when one has to invoke a particular query depending on the output of a previous query. These are kinds of automated tasks using SQL Triggers are handy in highly concurrent (busy) applications.

3. SQL Stored Procedures

Optimizing the number of lines of code is essential to improve productivity and to reduce throughput time. One of the factors that influence the number of lines of code is the size of SQL queries. Stored

Procedures can significantly reduce the number of lines of code required by SQL queries. They are modular functions that can be called from anywhere with specified parameters. With stored procedures, the code becomes modular and reusable.

4. SQL Aggregate Functions

Aggregate functions help programmers to perform operations on an array of data in a column. They can operate simultaneously on multiple rows. An example for aggregate function is 'average()'. This function, when applied on an array of columns, the result would be a computed average of all the values.

In the absence of such a function, the business layer programmer has to compute average using following steps.

1) Firstly, the programmer has to count the number of columns to be operated on.

2) Secondly, the programmer has to strip out null values from the selected columns.

3) Finally he has to calculate average using mathematical formulas.

CHAPTER 10: SQL INJECTION ATTACK

Users of computer systems and visitors to websites are familiar with authenticating their identity, or proving, "they are who they say they are," by entering their Username and Password.

What actually happens when you enter text into the Username and Password fields of a login screen is that the text is usually inserted or encapsulated into a SQL command.

This command checks the data you've entered against the information stored in the database, such as user names and their respective passwords. If your input matches what is stored in the database then you are granted access to the system.

If not, you get an error message and a chance to re-enter the correct information or you are refused entirely.

Databases are at the core of a modern organization's computer systems because they allow you to control your business processes. They store data needed to deliver specific content to visitors, customers, suppliers, and employees.

User credentials, financials, payment information, and company statistics may all reside within a database that can be accessed by legitimate users and unfortunately attackers as well. SQL or Structured Query Language is the computer language that allows you to store, manipulate, and retrieve data stored in the database

SQL injection is the exploitation of a website or computer system that is caused by the processing of invalid data that is entered into the form fields by a malicious user.

SQL injection can be used by an attacker to introduce (or "inject") code into a computer program to change the course of execution in order to access and manipulate the database behind the site, system or application.

SQL Injection vulnerabilities arise because the fields available for user input allow SQL statements to pass through to the database directly in order to process data and user requests.

If the input is not filtered properly, web applications may allow SQL commands that enable hackers to view unauthorized information from the database or even wipe it out.

The attack takes advantage of improper coding of web-based

applications and computer networks that incorporates features that deliver dynamic content such as:

- Login pages
- Customer support pages
- Product request forms
- Feedback forms
- Search pages
- Shopping carts

When the legitimate user submits his details, a SQL query is generated from these details and submitted to the database for verification. Using SQL Injection, the hacker may input specifically crafted SQL commands with the intent of bypassing the form barrier and seeing what lies behind it.

Many times all an attacker needs to perform a SQL Injection hacking attack is a web browser, knowledge of SQL queries, and creativity to guess important table and field names.

A simple illustration of a SQL injection attack goes like this; an attacker attempts compromise a system that they have no access to by entering code instead of their credentials.

So when the attacker is prompted to enter their Username and Password he enters codes such as 'x'='x'. And depending how the system's software is written, this command will be True because x always equal x, so the Username and Password combination will always be True or match!

Once an attacker realizes that a system is vulnerable to SQL Injection, he is able to inject SQL Commands through the input field. This allows the attacker to execute any SQL command on the database, including modifying, copying, and deleting data.

CHAPTER 11: HOW TO PREVENT DISASTROUS SQL INJECTION ATTACKS

The number one security topic present in applications that use PHP is the SQL injection. This is because PHP allows for web developers to make unfortunate mistakes when it comes to creating their SQL queries. But thankfully, fixing the problem is easy: all that is necessary is a few tips in security.

SQL injections are defined by the vulnerability in the SQL query that PHP developers make use of. When the developer in question puts forth an SQL query, he or she needs to make an effort to validate any input that could come from any web form or entry field. A simple input statement such as "a' OR 'a'='a'" could compromise the security of one's database with ease.

PHP developers have used the magic quotes function to help

safeguard against SQL injections. Magic quotes are no longer in use, however, since they were more of a hassle than anything.

It is recommended that if a developer has used magic quotes, he or she should remove them since they are no longer supported as of PHP 6. Thus, we need to look elsewhere for a security solution.

Using the "mysql_real_escape_string()" function will enable web developers to escape quotes properly. And unlike magic quotes, this function will only escape quotes that we need. Keep in mind that when using this function, it may be necessary to use the "striplslashes()" function to counteract the slashes that are being outputted as a result.

Another good way to prevent SQL injections is to simply restrict authority in SQL users where possible. For instance: it would be a good idea to create individual users that do specific things: such as create a table or update rows in the said table.

This can help make the task of ruining one's hard work much harder for malicious web users, although it's a lot more work for webmasters (Although well worth it).

It should be noted that programs and web applications that stop

SQL injections should not be obtained- since they commonly cost quite a bit of money.

As long as webmasters take precautions with what they create, there should be no reason to spend hundreds of dollars on software that only makes use of escape characters and formatting data correctly. This type of application is created to con webmasters into buying something they don't need- so dont fall victim to them!

Security is a big topic among webmasters, who make no money and achieve no fame by getting attacked via an SQL injection. To keep profits running high, it is recommended that webmasters make use of the tips previously mentioned.

It's also good to brush up on more PHP security tips, as well as make use of SQL injection scanners that are available over the Internet.

Security is a major concern for any web application. As experts say, no web application can be 100 % secure but we can surely try to minimize the security threats. SQL injection is just one area where your web application can be venerable. In this article I will concentrate on SQL injection

Database, is an integral part of any dynamic web site, where we store the product information, user information, and many more. This stored data some time can be of very sensitive nature like address, email, or sometime financial details.

It is the responsibility of the web site company to protect this data from being stolen. Using SQL injection, someone can corrupt this data or steal it or if the data is not fully protected then it can be even deleted.

SQL injection rely on the SQL queries that you perform on your database. A hacker will try to inject his own SQL script in the SQL query that you execute against your database. Suppose you allow your visitors to search for products on your website, someone can embed SQL script in the product description that you expect them to enter.

So when you are going to search your database for that description, you are in fact executing the hacker's sql script along with your search script. As I said before, this injected SQL script can be of very very serious nature.

Now to protect your application against SQL injection, you need to avoid using the simply concatenate SQL query and you should try to use parameterized SQL query. The parameters in a SQL query are considered the values for a single column and they cannot be executed as an independent SQL script.

There are many other ways to protect against SQL injection but parameterized query will provide your application the much needed security.

CHAPTER 12: SQL SERVER MONITORING

Server monitoring is important to maintain privacy and secrecy of company's records. As a huge amount of crucial data is stored in the server, so it is not a choice but a compulsion for an IT entrepreneur to install a server monitoring program to prevent his sensitive data from being discovered by the prying eyes.

Apart from protecting multiple layers of your database, a monitoring program also ensures inaccessibility of your record to the hackers. Considering the rising incidence of cyber crimes, it definitely gives you a peace of mind that your important database is beyond the reach of the cyber goons. It is this context where SQL server monitor claims a deserving mention.

A good SQL server monitor software must have the requisite qualities which work to the advantage of a corporate structure. While purchasing monitoring software, make sure that it caters to your requirements and provides the real time transaction stats.

Applications Manager SQL monitoring software is of great help for the database administrators as far as performance monitoring is concerned. Being an agent-less monitoring solution, it provides unmatched performance metrics to ensure that your SQL server runs smoothly and efficiently.

Applications manager manages a lot that speaks volume for its out-of-the-pattern performance. The web client of the application manager plays a significant role by helping you envisage as well as manage MSSQL server database. The web client also provides in-detail and in-depth data monitor.

This feature helps you make an educated choice regarding plan capacity, usage pattern and also generate a warning signal in the event of impending problems. And now there is the Root Cause Analysis which offers its helping hand to the server database administrator for the purpose of troubleshooting the performance problems.

The 'Grouping Capability' is an add-on feature which helps to group a database on the basis of supported business procedures. Such a facility helps the operations team to attach priority to the received alarms.

SQL Server Monitoring More to Offer:

SQL server is able to juggle many hats at the same point of time. It is fitted with some useful features which are capable of connecting to the database source and monitor varied system table column values.

Data collection and notification through alarms are also managed by the SQL monitor program. Memory usage, cache details, database details, connection statistics and SQ statistics are some important factors which are taken good care of in SQL database as a part of the monitoring program.

Additional offer for the SQL server monitoring software users - Applications Manager uses the Database Query Monitoring capability to monitor SQL Query of a MS SQL database. On strength of this added feature, a database administrator can monitor custom database and additional performance matrices.

Moreover, this additional offering can expose Business Metrics to Line of Business Managers. As security is your top priority, so you will surely not mind spending a little extra for a successful SQL server monitor application

CONCLUSION

Protecting your SQL databases can mean saving thousands for your company in terms of ensuring productivity, meeting regulation requirements, and preventing downtime and data loss.

Here are a few tips and tricks to ensure that your SQL databases are deployed correctly and available when the data is needed most.

In addition to the data itself, a SQL server includes the transaction log as well as the system databases. Both must be carefully protected if the application is going to be smoothly restored.

Watch Your Workloads Around Backup Windows

SQL backups can be performed while users are actively querying the database and transactions are being processed. SQL backups utilize a lot of system resources, especially I/O, so it's best to perform intensive, full backups when the system is experiencing light load times.

Shorten Data Backups

If overall performance is suffering due to long backup windows, several measures can be taken to reduce the time that the system is performing a backup. One way to shorten is to backup to disk.

If you're backing up to disk before offloading to another backup system, take care to not backup to the same disk that is used to store the database or transaction.

Copying the database to a separate array can prevent I/O overload as well as ensure the database is available in the event of a primary system failure.

Use Different Backup Methods

SQL server offers different backup methods-full, differential, and transaction backups. There are built into the SQL server. Choosing the back-up method depends largely on your environment. Specifically, it depends on how large the database it is and how critical the database is to your business.

Full backups can weigh down your servers and storage systems, so plan carefully how often you need to perform a full backup versus differential or transactional backups.

Small databases that are not too large and change infrequently can be backed up only daily or weekly. Transactional databases that are mission critical should be backup up as often as possible.

Backup Transaction Logs Frequently

Next to the database, transaction logs are the most important data in a SQL server database. The log covers activity and can be used to perform PiT (point-in-time) restorations.

Remember: the transactional backup only backs up to the last transactional backup, so a full restore may mean performing a series of transactional backups in order to fully resort the database.

The transactional log should be performed every ten minutes for extremely active databases, and at least several times a day.

Backing Up SQL System Databases

The system databases are the other vital component of a SQL server application, including both msdb and master. There contain essential data such as system configuration and are necessary in the event of a complete restore.

However, the system databases change less frequently and should be backed up at least weekly, or daily if it is a particularly active database.

One of the greatest factors that affects performance and protection of the Microsoft SQL server is the I/O of the disk subsystem.

Backups and Storage Growth

Multiple backups can create significant storage costs as full, differential, and transactional backups are performed for active SQL systems on a regular basis. Here are a few ways to control costs, and ensure the data is properly backed up.

Offload backups to a separate, low-cost storage array. This practice ensures high-performance, high-cost disk is freed up for active databases.

 Planning for growth up-front can prevent expensive, last minutes storage purchases.

When purchasing a storage array from Reliant Technology, your storage consultant will help you properly forecast your database growth and ensure you have enough low-cost, high-capacity disk to properly protect system and transactional logs for your databases.